CHRISTIANITY AND PHILOSOPHY

I V P *Series in Contemporary Christian Thought*

Christianity
and
Philosophy
by
Arthur F. Holmes

Director of Philosophy
Wheaton College

Inter-Varsity Press • Chicago 10

Library of Congress catalog card number: 60-13076

Cover design by Jack Sidebotham

Printed in the United States of America

Preface

THE RELATIONSHIP of faith and reason concerned the earliest Christians as they encountered the intellectual environment of the Roman Empire. It has concerned Christian thinkers of every age as they sought to develop a Christian philosophy in relation to prevailing currents of thought.

The issue of faith and reason has taken on renewed significance in the face of new attitudes toward both Christianity and philosophy. The influence of Soren Kierkegaard and religious existentialism on the one hand, and the approach of the new analytic philosophy on the other, raise questions about the meaningfulness as well as the validity of religious assertions.

The Christian student today is forced to face the problem of faith and reason in new terms, as the philosophical atmosphere of our universities has been conditioned by these recent movements. He must do this not only for his own understanding of Christianity, but also for effective communication of the gospel.

As an aid in this task, it is a pleasure to present this booklet by Professor Arthur F. Holmes. The author first sets forth the essence and purpose of philosophy. He then proceeds to explain the nature of Christianity and to relate it to the philosophic enterprise. In developing his thought, Professor Holmes has drawn upon his years of experience at Northwestern University where he received his Ph.D., his teaching of philosophy at Wheaton College, and his association with Inter-Varsity camps and conferences where he has come increasingly to understand the problems students face in this realm.

Professor Holmes sets forth the basic issues clearly and in such a way that the general reader may easily grasp the over-all relationship between Christianity and philosophy. The student who is interested in pursuing the subject further will find that the following pages serve as an excellent introduction, with guideposts for additional study.

Christianity and Philosophy is the first in a series of booklets on contemporary Christian thought by the Inter-Varsity Press. This series deals with crucial issues and influential thinkers in the current encounter of Christianity with the world that has been termed *post-Christian.* May it be of help in demonstrating that the Christian faith is still a live option for the thinking student who grapples with the basic problems of a world so often described in terms of meaninglessness and despair.

CHARLES E. HUMMEL

Contents

Introduction

TWENTIETH-CENTURY Christianity faces a pagan world. While Marxist concepts dominate the larger part of the Eurasian landmass with its vast populations, other intellectual descendants of nineteenth-century German thinkers vie for the attention of the western mind in general and Christianity in particular. As a result, there constantly appear attempted rapprochements between Christianity and idealism, Christianity and existentialism, Christianity and positivism, and so forth. The concepts of myth and paradox strive to replace those of analogy and mystery; the possibility of meaningful religious language again evokes discussion.

First-century Christianity itself was born into a philosophically minded pagan culture. Alexander the Great had sought to impose Greek thought patterns on the eastern mediterranean world; Antiochus Epiphanes attempted to do the same with the Jews; and Rome triumphed in the East only to be consumed by the octopus-like tentacles of Hellenism. Consequently, early Christianity confronted a philosophically minded Greco-Roman world, and was nurtured by a Judaism that had its Hellenists as well as its culturally isolationist Pharisees. From its earliest years, therefore, the Church was compelled to come to grips with a question that has proved perennial and which yet challenges it: the relationship of Christianity to philosophy.

The Church's perennial interest in the question has taken a variety of forms. Some individuals and groups, suspicious either of philosophic infiltration into theology, or else of the soul-callousing effect of intellectualism, repudiated philosophy as intrinsically unchristian. Others, impressed by parallels between the statements of certain philosophers and those of the Jewish and Christian Scriptures, uncritically embraced as essentially Christian not only the philosophic enterprise but also particular philosophic viewpoints and conclusions. Others again, recognizing the legitimacy of what philosophers try to do but not of everything they have done, attempted to work out syntheses that would preserve the final authority of divine revelation.

The twentieth-century Christian who examines the record cannot avoid the conclusion that the main stream of historic orthodoxy has followed neither of the first two avenues, has been neither obscurantist nor rationalist. He is compelled to develop for himself a working relationship between Christianity and philosophy that will discredit neither Christianity nor philosophy. Basic to this task is an understanding of the nature of the two enterprises involved. All too often the repudiation of philosophy, whether by significant writers or by popular Christian sentiment, stems from a failure to appreciate what philosophers are actually trying to do. With similar frequency the rationalistic rejection or compromise of the faith stems from a failure to appreciate the full intent and broad relevance of Christianity.

What follows is, then, an attempt to introduce and

2]

in a sense to explore the historic problem of reason and revelation in its contemporary setting, by trying to understand the nature of philosophy and Christianity respectively. In its brief compass it can do no more; it can hope to be suggestive, but neither exhaustive nor conclusive.

I. What Is Philosophy?

PYTHAGORAS was supposedly the first to call himself a philosopher. In coining this designation he intended to use it literally: the philosopher is a "lover of wisdom." Two implications have remained true of subsequent philosophy. First, it involves one in a persistent and resolute quest that refuses to be satisfied with glib answers and oversimplified solutions. Second, its goal of wisdom, *sophia*, brooks neither idle curiosity nor a coldly impersonal amassing of irrelevant information. Rather, it is concerned with man's basic questions because they bear on his attainment to "the good life," regardless of whether this good is to be found in the study of ultimate reality, in understanding man, in knowing God, or in a life of responsible citizenship.

The popular concept of a "philosophy of life" makes sense in this context. It suggests a reflective outlook

[3

which controls our reactions to life's vicissitudes and guides our choices between its innumerable paths. In kindred fashion we speak of taking reverses "philosophically," that is to say, with a patience born of mature reflection upon all that life offers.

These, however, are popular rather than technical usages. While they illustrate the combination of thoughtful reflection and practical concern, they are still more representative of the homespun ideas of the man-in-the-street than of the interests of the professional philosopher.

The Nature of Philosophy

Philosophy is characterized not so much by its distinctive subject matter as by its objectives and methods. The ancients included all known disciplines within the general pale of philosophy, and less than a century ago the natural sciences were still called "natural philosophy." It must not be supposed, therefore, that present-day philosophers are unconcerned about the subject matter of other disciplines. They are concerned with it, however, in a different way than are physical or social scientists. They are concerned with the critical examination of scientific methods, of general concepts that arise or are assumed, of the interrelationship of various disciplines.

The professional philosopher has customarily pursued either or both of two objectives that have crystallized since the days of Pythagoras. These are, first, a comprehensive world view and, second, clarity of understanding.

1. The quest for a comprehensive world view is the aspect of philosophy most in question in discussions of its bearing on Christianity. Sometimes called systematic or speculative philosophy, it suggests a carefully developed, coherent explanation of the nature of God, man, and the universe that embraces as far as possible all the known interrelationships that arise. Comparatively few philosophers have succeeded in working out enduring world views. The names of Aristotle and Hegel stand as two of the greatest by virtue of both their encyclopedic and their systematizing work.

The very quest for a world view raises problems which have not escaped the penetrating vision of the less venturesome. The scope of human knowledge is at best limited, and even the vast mass of scientific insight accumulated since the Renaissance seems likely to be but a tiny glimpse of otherwise unimagined vistas. Even the trustworthiness of human knowledge is open to question: social ideologies and scientific hypotheses alike suffer emendation; a man's understanding is inevitably relative to his position in space and his perspective in history; it is open to debate whether man will ever apprehend more than passing phenomena that deceptively shadow unknowable realities. Is it any wonder, it is argued, that world views come and go with their respective cultures, reflecting as they must a changing *Zeitgeist?* A truly comprehensive world-and-life view presupposes that we see the *whole* of life

[5

steadily and unchangeably. It presupposes the humanly impossible—the viewpoints and abilities of Deity.

Inevitably, therefore, the systematic philosopher cannot claim to have developed a final and exhaustive world view. But he can lay claim to the quest for a system that builds upon lessons from the past and upon present intimations of the future. He makes a persistent *attempt* to see life as totally and as steadily as is humanly possible, an attempt that admits to fallible interpretations and unsolved problems, yet strives constantly for that self-consistency which is a hallmark of truth.

Even this fails to satisfy modern objectors. What is known must be intelligible, and if intelligible, then communicable. Is human language adequate to the task? Can logic, syntax, and verbal symbols capture and convey the unity and diversity of those multidimensioned realities that lie around man and beyond? Or must man forego the right to anything which evades statistical and experimental procedures? The quest for a world view today supposes that questions such as these have been satisfactorily answered. It is little wonder that, in most philosophical circles, logically prior issues such as these dominate the scene—that philosophy's second objective has risen to the fore.

2. The quest for clarity of understanding is by no means the innovation of twentieth-century philosophical analysts. While it is true that the anti-metaphysical temper of the contemporary mind has served to reemphasize problems of meaning, to some extent conceptual, logical, or linguistic analysis and criticism have been the perennial concern of philosophers. Socrates

was a classical example; with his renowned dialectical method he sought for unambiguous expression based on a clear understanding of questions and concepts. The Socratic dialogues are masterpieces of analysis, brilliantly probing minds in the quest for meaning and truth.

By the same token it is significant that Socrates stimulated the more systematic genius of Plato and Aristotle. The clarification of individual questions introduced still others, and these in turn raised issues of a more general and inclusive nature. Analysis became the prelude to system-building. So it has been since. Scholastic analyses of questions regarding God and man, nature and grace, produced the neo-Aristotelian system of Thomas Aquinas. Enlightenment analyses of the problem of knowledge, stimulated by the growth of physical sciences, generated the world views of the nineteenth century.

The quests for clarity and consistency, then, go hand in hand. If consistency is the logical desideratum of a world view, then clarity is the rational desideratum of the quest for understanding. Other requirements may indeed be involved of an empirical, psychological, or even cultural nature, but in these two desiderata one finds indispensable criteria of the rational. Philosophy, as a rational activity, pursues both clarity and consistency. Its quest is for both a lucid understanding and a comprehensive world view. It is for this reason that either deliberately or unintentionally obscured notions are as objectionable as ultimate self-contradictions. It is for this reason also that philosophy can claim to be a legitimate enterprise: its objectives are essentially those of all rational beings.

It should be recognized, however, that philosophy remains a quest. As long as man's insight is finite, elements of mystery are liable to shroud his otherwise clear understanding. He may probe the data and analyze both concepts and language, but he does so in the *quest* for a degree of clarity that for the present remains elusive. In addition, as long as the scope of man's knowledge is limited, and as long as his systematic reasoning must employ guiding hypotheses and basic presuppositions which admit of no demonstrative certainty, the possibility of error threatens an otherwise consistent position. He may include a greater scope of learning, may reassess his presuppositions and check his logic, but he does so still in the *quest* for the kind of a system that for the present eludes him. Philosophy is a quest with which dogmatism, cynicism, and obscurantism are all equally incompatible.

The Function of Philosophy

The philosophical quest may be legitimate but does it serve any useful purpose in society? To the man-in-the-street, and for the Christian seeking to develop a working relationship to philosophy, the question is crucial. A legitimate but valueless enterprise can merit little respect.

Philosophy is but one phase of human culture. Culture as a whole is the developed pattern of human life as it centers around certain key values. Philosophy seeks to clarify this value-structure and to express it in a systematic world-and-life view. It is culture becoming self-critical and systematically reflective. It is a process of intellectual maturation analogous to that of individuals. The child who cries for the moon wants the yellow ball he sees on the roof of the house next door. The adolescent laughs at his little brother, but finds in the full moon a stimulus to romance and an occasion for fun. The adult, however, sees an object of aesthetic enjoyment or scientific investigation. Intellectual maturation, whether in the individual or in the group, involves a refining of ideas, a re-expression of ideals, a careful sifting of naive notions. Childhood assumptions give way to adolescent attitudes, and these in turn develop into adult viewpoints.

In a maturating culture philosophy provides an intellectual conscience to probe existing thought-patterns, and it develops an over-all world view as a guide in the processes and conflicts of history.

Socrates exemplifies the first function of philosophy, that of an intellectual conscience for society. Disgusted by political intrigue, concerned about moral relativism, alarmed at signs of cultural disintegration, he sought to expose underlying confusions of mind, to force the development of clear ideas, to encourage the pursuit of true values. In rejecting Socrates, Athens repressed its intellectual conscience. Subsequent philosophers have to various extents served the same function. Philosophical criticism compelled the early church to clarify its understanding of the Trinity. Philosophical insistence on a clear understanding of man forced the development of Renaissance political theories which molded democratic ideals. Intellectual confusion is a hazard to the whole of human society, a hazard against which the quest for clear understanding stands guard.

The philosopher-king of Plato's *Republic* illustrates the second cultural function of philosophy, the development of a guiding world view. Plato supposes that the reflective individual, who has gained for himself a clear understanding of true values, will have gained a proper perspective on the down-to-earth issues of daily life. He will approach decisions neither emotively nor with a partisan spirit, but in the light of his over-all view of man and his place in the universe. His world view will enable him to rule well.

This ideal admittedly did not prove too practicable. Contingent circumstances, political intrigue, and corruption paid scanty respect to Plato's lofty idealism. Yet he touched upon the indubitable fact that a developed world view is an indispensable guide not only for the individual but also for society. It is philosophy which provides world views. In content and acceptability they vary. Marx and Nietzsche, Dewey and Hegel, Locke and Rousseau, Augustine and Aquinas, each has molded history by developing ideologies that guided culture.

Philosophy, then, is a momentous undertaking that cannot be ignored and must not be underestimated. Its twofold quest endows it with a twofold cultural mission. The problem of revelation and reason must be considered in this context. Christians face a pagan culture in which varied philosophic forces are at work. Christianity's relationship to philosophy will accordingly depend at least in part on Christianity's relationship to human culture.

II. What Is Christianity?

THE CHRISTIAN message begins with an all-important diagnosis of the nature and need of man. It is addressed to man as a rational being capable of understanding communicated ideas, as a moral being responsible for his own decisions and actions. Rationality and morality are traits of personality and it is this which characterizes the image of God in man, making him unique in creation and equipping him for that intercourse with other personalities which has produced human culture. It makes possible man's highest good, not culture, but the knowledge of and a personal fellowship with God. The image of God in man is marred by sin; his understanding is obscured and his morality debased. As a result the individual, the group, and their cultural achievements all suffer.

Christianity claims that God enlightens the sinner's understanding by an historical process of revelation climaxing in the Incarnation of Jesus Christ, and that He remedies moral failure through the personal redemp-

[11

tion provided by the Incarnate Christ. Because of the impact of God's revelation and redemption on their thinking and living, Christians have had, as we shall observe, a distinctive impact upon the culture of their day. Christianity may therefore be defined as that religion of revelation and redemption which centers in the divine person and historic work of Jesus Christ.

This definition requires further explication. We shall first explore the genus—it is a religion—and then the differentia—revelation and redemption centering in Jesus Christ.

Christianity as a Religion

Philosophy is one phase of human culture. Religion is another. Religion is not to be equated with philosophy. A particular religion is not itself a philosophy. Both its goals and its methods are different.

Philosophy clarifies and systematizes the dominant ideas and values of men. Religion preserves and in some cases originates them. Religious experience, both corporate and individual, reinforces beliefs and commitments and provides something of the dynamic which integrates personalities and unifies culture. By suggesting that man's *raison d'être* lies outside himself, it points to values that transcend the changing moods and scenes of the present struggle.

Generalizations such as these are familiar to anthropologists and to philosophers of religion. They need to be noted; for while Christianity may indeed be unique among religions, it is still a religion, and as such it is concerned with the values around which a culture is structured and a philosophy developed. Christianity points men to "the good life," enjoyed both here and hereafter through the knowledge of God. "What is the chief end of man?" asks the Westminster Shorter Catechism. It is "to glorify God and to enjoy Him forever." Christian experience, both corporate and individual, reinforces this belief and renews one's commitment to its various implications. It provides something of the dynamic which integrates the believer's life and unifies the Christian community. In the so-called "Christian" nations, those, that is, which have most felt the impact of the Judeo-Christian tradition, Christians have played their part in the structuring of culture. As members of society they inevitably helped build the culture. As Christians they inevitably built into it some of the ideas and values rooted in their knowledge of God. Clement and Augustine, Luther and Calvin, Wesley and Wilberforce all played their part. Directly or indirectly they and others had a hand, therefore, in the development of the philosophies of their day and ours.

The Differentia of Christianity

Christianity is a revealed religion; that is to say, it is the product, not of man's ordinary insights into his relationship to God—what we speak of as natural religion—but of God's special revelation of Himself. The Old Testament records God's self-manifestation in the history of Israel and the experience of believers, as well as in the utterances of His prophets. The New Testament records God's activity in the development of the early Church, its doctrine and its conduct. But the knowledge of God provided and attested by the Biblical record is most dramatically presented in Jesus Christ. The entire Bible makes it clear that God's supreme self-revelation occurred in the person and work of His Incarnate Son. The Christian revelation centers in the One who claimed, "He that hath seen Me hath seen the Father."

From its earliest days the Church has regarded Scripture as its final and sufficient rule of faith and practice. Biblical teachings about God and man, sin and grace, personal and social ethics have given direction to believers' reflection on the revelation, and so guided their theology and philosophy. The Christian revelation is intended to lead man to know God in terms of the objective truth he learns from Scripture. It is transmitted to man by the vehicle of human language, in a body of literature inspired by the Holy Spirit. For this reason the Biblical scholar engages in textual criticism—in order to ensure an accurate text; he engages in grammatical and historical exegesis—in order to ascertain the intent of the writer's statements; he enters upon every literary science that aids clear and correct understanding of divine revelation.

One caution is necessary at this point. The revelation which brings men to a knowledge of God is not exclusively objective. John Calvin spoke of the inner testimony of the Holy Spirit; Augustine had called it "illumination"; Scripture insists that spiritual truths only become personally relevant when impressed upon the mind by God's Spirit. The seed must germinate and

14]

take root if it is to produce fruit. But the necessity of a subjective work of God denies neither the objectivity of the truth nor the demand for a careful, rational study of Scripture. It means, rather, that the Holy Spirit operates in conjunction with normal mental processes so as to make the truth meaningful to the individual. In all His works God employs the natural processes He has ordained.

To know God is man's highest good. Man is kept from this knowledge not only by his ignorance, willful or otherwise, but also by his sin. His moral condition confuses his understanding and hampers both faith and fellowship. He needs not only the revelation but also the redemption provided by the divine person and historic work of Jesus Christ.

Redemption, too, has both objective and subjective sides. The former is seen in the historical work of the Savior in His life on earth, His crucifixion and His resurrection. The latter is seen in the subjective work of the Holy Spirit in transforming the believer—that which theology speaks of as regeneration and sanctification. One may know about God through revelation, but one may only gain a saving knowledge and enter into personal fellowship with Him on the basis of redemption and its transforming effect on the moral life and spiritual outlook. The effect is pervasive. Attitudes to nature and society, to intellectual and emotional involvements, to the state and the family, are alike involved. The Christian brings Christian ideas and values to his culture. He brings the potential for a Christian world view.

The Truth–Claims of Christianity

Christianity claims to be true. Its truth-claims extend to all Biblical assertions, those concerning God and man, the history of Israel and the historical Incarnation, miraculous events and supernaturalist doctrines.

The claim to truth arouses objections. What have metaphysics, history, and miracle to do with Christianity? Since the days of Kant it has become customary either to subordinate truth-claims to value-judgments, or to regard truth as changing and relative, or else to reduce it to the subjective emotive intensity of an existential experience. In any case Christianity is either compromised by or divorced from the "truth" in other cultural areas—history, science or philosophy.

Three observations seem pertinent in the interests of establishing a relationship between Christianity and philosophy that will compromise neither Christianity nor philosophy. First, it should be observed at this stage that because of inevitable limitations on human knowledge, there will remain areas of problem and mystery. We shall return to this point in the final chapter. Second, the doctrine of twofold truth in either its old or its new forms is not ultimately satisfying to either the philosopher or the theologian. It has been the position of historic Christianity that truth is one. What is historically untrue or logically contradictory can neither possess religious value nor make theological sense. Error is error and nonsense is nonsense in every realm of thought. Problems there may be, attesting the finite-

ness of human understanding, but irreconcilable para-
doxes there cannot be if they attest the inconsistency of
God and the irrationality of His universe. If God cannot
contradict Himself, neither can general revelation contradict special revelation, neither can scientific data
contradict Biblical data, and neither can valid philosophical reasoning contradict valid theological reasoning. Just as a careful logic cannot allow contradictory
truths without forfeiting the laws of thought, so a consistent theism cannot allow contradictory truths without
forfeiting the veracity of God. Rather, when problems
arise, the data are incomplete or misunderstood, or else
the reasoning processes are fallacious or inconclusive.

God is the ultimate source of all knowledge, and His
knowledge provides the ultimate standard of all truth.
Augustine insisted on this and argued further that one
cannot reason himself out of reason. Nor, we may add,
can one consistently plead for the allowing of inconsistencies. An understanding of Christianity argues that
truth is one, and that a working relationship between
Christianity and philosophy can best be developed on
this premise. On the contrary, those post-Kantian movements such as positivism, Ritschlianism, and existentialism which make a disjunction between fact and value,
science and religion, or reason and faith, and which
thereby relegate Christianity to the extra- or supra-logi-
cal, are both self-destructive from the viewpoint of
logical consistency and incompatible with historic
Christianity.

Our third observation regarding the truth-claims of
Christianity is that while the essence of Christian faith

[17

is a total and continuing commitment to God in Christ, yet it involves the believer in a commitment to certain objective truths and historical facts understood in clear-cut ways.

Enlightenment writers tended to speak of faith as an emotive response devoid of any rationale. What could not be understood might be believed. What could not be demonstrated might be "accepted on faith." This view is both psychologically and Biblically inadequate. In the first place, faith must have a known object. Beliefs have cognitive content. It is for this reason that the Church has always endeavored to clarify by its preaching and teaching those truths to which a response is sought. Faith that is totally devoid of understanding is more like the behavioral response of an animal than genuine belief. Paul said, "I know whom I have believed." In the second place, faith involves a rationale. It is no blind leap in the dark. It gives "a reason for the hope" it prizes. Beginning with its earliest apologists the Church has adduced evidences of varied sorts in vindication of its claims. Faith that involves clear ideas and a significant rationale cannot be purely emotive. What then is it?

The Bible makes no disjunction between head and heart. A careful study of the term "heart" in Scripture unfolds its evident meaning: the ruling center of the entire personality. Rational functions are ascribed to the heart more than are emotive functions. To say that a man believes "in his heart," then, asserts that he is committed at the very roots of his life. To be a "wholehearted" believer is to be totally committed. Similarly

18]

the Biblical picture of faith, given under such metaphors as accepting, following, eating, and drinking, suggests complete participation, a life-commitment. Verbal assent alone is not faith; faith must issue in a new texture of life. What is needed is "faith that works by love." Theologians therefore speak of faith as committing the entire person to God, not only his "religious" activities but all of his values and ideas—the rational as well as the emotive aspects of his life.

Faith is a function of the entire personality. Early martyrs died rather than renounce their beliefs, because that would have retracted their total commitment. The early Church formulated the Apostles' Creed as a statement of basic truths to be subscribed to by all purported converts. Total Christian faith inevitably commits one to objective truths pertaining to metaphysics (*I believe in God the Father Almighty, Maker of heaven and earth*), to the miraculous (*born of the Virgin Mary,* etc.), to history (*suffered under Pontius Pilate*), and to morals (*He shall come to judge the quick and the dead*).

It is impossible to mistake the intent of the early Christians. Fact and value, objective truth and subjective experience were wholly inseparable within their one total commitment of faith in Jesus Christ. Vital faith and rational contemplation are not the antithetical states supposed by Kierkegaard. It is not a case of either/or. To regard the crisis of faith as simply a confrontation by the Inscrutable or an attainment to authentic existence is as fallacious as to regard it as simply a mental assent to historical facts or objective truths. Faith integrates both subjective and objective factors.

This, in fact, is the genius of genuine Christian faith—that it commits the believer wholeheartedly to One about whose person and work he gained clear-cut and reasonable convictions. To this the spirited controversies of apostolic, patristic, and reformation days bear abundant witness. Faith is a clearheaded involvement.

Christianity then is not a religion of culturally irrelevant vagaries. It appeals for a faith so complete that it will make possible not only a clear mental formulation of Christian ideas and values, but also a vital experience that remolds both men and culture. Christianity is a religion, not a philosophy; but as a religion it seeks to redeem both the men who do philosophy and the culture that shapes them. Its effect upon philosophy is both inevitable and pervasive. It is a momentous movement that cannot be ignored and must not be underestimated.

III. Christianity and Philosophy

IN THE foregoing pages it has been suggested that philosophy, as historically seen and practised, pursues two objectives which provide it with a twofold function in human culture. The quest for clear understanding makes philosophy something of an intellectual conscience; the quest for a world view lends perspec-

tives that guide the development of other phases of
culture. It has been further suggested that Christianity
as historically seen and practised proclaims a message
centering in the person and work of Jesus Christ. While
it teaches that the intended impact of revelation and
redemption is contingent upon the subjective work of
God's Spirit in the individual believer, it also affirms
certain objective truths and historical facts. These ob-
viously provide a point of contact between Christianity
and philosophy. What further can be said as to the relationship between these two enterprises as we have come
to understand them?

Variant Attitudes

History reveals a variety of approaches to the question. Each reflects its own milieu and each, we suggest,
could be examined in the light of its understanding of
Christianity and philosophy respectively. That the relationship we posit between the two depends on our
understanding of each is a truism.

The approach which repudiates philosophy as intrinsically un-Christian was epitomized in antiquity by
Tertullian of Carthage. Born around 160 A.D., trained
as a lawyer, converted to Christianity in his early thir-
ties, he was an ardent and somewhat impetuous apologist. In his reaction against the encroachments of
Gnostic rationalism, Tertullian branded philosophy as
futile and destructive, and seems to have relished the
apparent irrationality of certain Christian beliefs. Ob-
viously he failed to criticize his own use of reason,

[21

and note the indebtedness to philosophy that is evident in his use of the Stoics' traducian view regarding the origin of the human soul. The lesson is plain: to divorce oneself entirely from philosophy would be to detach faith from life, Christianity from culture. Fortunately, as Tertullian himself shows, this is impossible.

Yet subsequent history exhibits individuals with kindred, although perhaps less extreme, tendencies. Repulsed by Descartes' unbounded rationalistic optimism, Blaise Pascal followed Montaigne and the Greek sceptics in reasoning that metaphysical arguments are all equipollent. Philosophical argumentation is therefore irrelevant to Christianity. The only support the heart can find lies in the areas of historical evidences and miraculous attestations. Soren Kierkegaard recoiled from the rationalistic dogmatism of Hegel's relentlessly logical system. Philosophy, he asserted, is a presumptuous, ineffective, and dangerous substitute for spiritual vitality. Christian faith is characterized by paradox and absurdity. Many exponents of neo-orthodox theology adopt the same negative attitude.

It is difficult to determine, however, in which sense Christianity could legitimately be regarded as irrational. If its doctrines defy clarification and its God lies hidden in the smog of total incomprehensibility, then traditional revelation-claims are denied. If its assertions are contrary to fact and its positions self-contradictory, then the veracity of God is reduced to a sheer equivocation. Yet, despite the dangers of these implications, they represent the alternatives embraced by many contemporary thinkers. The only alternative would be to assert

22]

the intelligibility and consistency of Christianity—in a word, its rationality, and this would reestablish its positive connection with the philosophic enterprise. Difficulties there may be in such a connection, but they are certainly no greater than those in the irrationalist position.

The second traditional approach to our problem is one which compromises the claims not of philosophy but of Christianity. The Christian Gnostics of patristic times provide classic examples. So desirous were they of integrating Christianity into prevalent thought-patterns that they forfeited the distinctives of the faith. Public, objective revelation was hidden in a secret *gnosis* unfolded to the intellegentsia alone. Some of the early apologists successfully resisted Gnosticism per se, only to exaggerate the similarities of Christianity and philosophy in other ways. Justin Martyr, for instance, virtually identifying John's *Logos* with those of Plato and the Stoics, inferred that all who live according to reason are Christians, Socrates and others included.

Similar cases could be cited from modern times. Descartes purported to be a revelational theist. But his rationalistic disregard for Christianity's distinctives led others to view supernatural revelation and redemption as unnecessary. Enlightenment deism resulted. Nineteenth-century liberal theology developed in similar style. Adolph Harnack, for instance, thought he detected admixtures of philosophy even in New Testament Christianity. In its conception and development, dogma was a "work of the Greek Spirit on the soil of the Gospel." The task of the Protestant critic, therefore, is to determine the spiritual core of Christianity that has proved so adaptable to varying philosophic demands. The task of the theologian is to inject Christian meaning into contemporary life by accommodating the spiritual core of Christianity to present cultural demands. The result is a Christianity devoid of both trustworthy revelation and personal redemption, as historically understood.

The third traditional approach attempts to synthesize faith and reason. Two historical syntheses provide the landmarks. Augustine of Hippo, combatting the Manichean rationalism from which he had been converted, recognized the indispensable contributions of the Christian revelation to his understanding. He also found a valuable ally in the Neoplatonism to which Bishop Ambrose had introduced him. Insisting that reason is a divine gift, he brought philosophy to the fight against sceptics and rationalists alike. Insisting that Christianity is a divine revelation, he presented it as the sure answer to man's intellectual and moral woes. Faith and reason, for him, are inseparably intertwined: each step of conscious faith inevitably involves some reasoning; and each process of reasoning consciously or unconsciously involves some act of faith. "Faith is understanding's step and understanding is faith's reward." Augustine's synthesis guided the thought of the Franciscans, later of Calvin and the present-day Reformed traditions.

Thomas Aquinas developed another synthesis, now the most widespread among Roman Catholic thinkers and frequently followed by non-Reformed Protestants. So impressed was he by Aristotle's valuable contribu-

24]

tions that Thomas came to regard the Christian revelation as supplementing rather than permeating true philosophical insights. Natural philosophy can demonstrate the premises of revealed theology: the existence of God and the immortality of the soul. But grace alone can introduce us to what lies beyond this line, where reason's task becomes one simply of explicating and systematizing revealed truths.

Contemporary evangelical thought on the subject tends to vary. At the one extreme, some exponents seem to the present writer to press Augustine into a Kierkegaardian position. At the Thomistic extreme, some so emphasize the unaided powers of human reason as to press towards a Cartesian position. Various gradations appear in between. Quite apparently, any attempt at a detailed construction would represent the writer's own interpretation of a given tradition. Such is not the present purpose. It is rather the intention to set up certain guideposts to enable the reader to explore further the basic problem involved.

The Basic Problem

Undergirding all questions concerning the relation of Christianity to philosophy lies the obvious fact that the Christian religion lives in a pagan culture and the obvious implication that it must without compromise adapt itself to the task of living in and communicating to that culture. If Christians are to understand, appreciate, and profit from their faith, they must be able to think about it in ways that they themselves find meaningful—ways shaped by their culture with its traditions, education, language, and philosophies. If Christians are to communicate their faith to others it must be in ways that are meaningful to those others, ways provided by the culture they share: traditions, education, language, philosophies, etc. The formulation of Christian theology, the transforming effect of the gospel on both the individual and the culture, the investigation of historical and literary materials—all such activities of the church attest this inevitable interaction. This much has already become apparent. Yet it must be understood more fully.

Biblical Examples

The first guidepost to such understanding is provided by New Testament examples of the relationship between Christianity and philosophy. The apostles both faced the problems and used the opportunities presented by the philosophies of their day. Three passages assume major significance: I Corinthians 1 and 2, Colossians, and John 1.

In I Corinthians Paul makes a distinction between the wisdom of the world and that of God. He asserts that the latter, not the former, leads man to the knowledge of God; that whereas the world scoffs at the revealed wisdom of God, the world's wisdom is really foolish by comparison. It should be observed that Paul is writing of his initial visit to Corinth following his experience with the Athenian philosophers (Acts 17). The Epicureans and Stoics of Athens were both naturalists, and even the Platonists would undoubtedly have

26]

joined in ridiculing the notion of a resurrection. To the Greek mind it was both undesirable and impossible. They preferred their rationalistic conclusions to the message of the Cross. In explaining this to the Corinthians, Paul points out that biases so deeply rooted in the thought-patterns of a culture ("the world") are not likely to be dispelled by counter-assertions alone, no matter how powerfully argued. Only the power of God can confound them; only the Spirit of God can instruct them effectively. *He* makes objective truth subjectively acceptable.

In the Colossian epistle Paul is combatting a heresy of the Gnostic variety. Rooted in a rationalistic epistemology, it presented a metaphysic that made Christ one of a series of emanations from God, and it taught a rigid asceticism as the way of salvation from an evil, material world. In reply the apostle postulates certain essentials of a Christian world view. He argues that Jesus Christ is the focus of all wisdom; he who knows Christ has learned the mystery that gives perspective to other truth. Christ is the Eternal Creator of the cosmos; he who knows Christ has gained direction for his metaphysical formulations. Christ is the crucified and risen Redeemer; he who knows Christ has found deliverance from the evil lurking in his own soul; he lives an exemplary life in all branches of society, motivated by devotion to Christ and guided by insight into life's highest values.

It should be observed that while Paul warns against a philosophy rooted exclusively in the principles and traditions of human culture, he nevertheless recognizes the possibility of philosophy being "after Christ" (2:8). Nor does he divorce his own Christian philosophizing from its cultural setting; rather he employs the terminology of the very movement to which he objects—terms such as "wisdom," "knowledge," "fullness," "mystery," and "philosophy" itself. Did he use such terminology with none of its original meaning, he would merely equivocate; the Gnostics would use a given term in sense *A* and he would use it in sense *B;* the two senses would have nothing in common; the word itself would convey nothing. Did he use their terminology uncritically and make predications akin to their own, then he and they would differ not at all. But by the skillful use of words in new contexts, he successfully modified their meanings while drawing sufficiently close analogies to make the necessary contact with cultural thought-patterns.

In the first chapter of his gospel, John uses the philosophical term, *Logos,* to describe Jesus Christ. Heraclitus had used it to refer to the order apparent in a world of change. The Stoics followed his example, rooting such order in an impersonal though rational cosmic force, a *Logos* that operated through its multiplied *logoi spermatikoi.* Philo, the Alexandrian Jew, identified this *Logos* with the *wisdom* of Hebrew literature, but certainly failed to regard it as a coequal person in an eternal Divine Trinity. John makes use of the same term. Undoubtedly he is primarily dependent on Old Testament parallels to the Greek concept. But he neither empties the Greek term of all cultural meaning nor uses it simply in any one of its previous meanings. He speaks of the *Logos* as both identical with God and distinguishable within the Godhead. He speaks of Him as the Personal Creator, the Source of both being and order. He asserts that this *Logos* became incarnate to reveal the Father and redeem men. This is another case of the adaptation of language and concepts as a means of orienting the Christian message in a pagan environment, a means employed ever since, whether in the Trinitarian formulations of the church fathers or the scholastic doctrine of analogy. Similar conclusions could be drawn from the treatment in I John of yet another variety of Gnosticism.

From these Biblical examples, then, we elicit the following principles:

1. In the final analysis the minds of men molded by pagan thought-patterns are won, not by philosophical argument or rhetorical device, but by the power of the Holy Spirit.

2. Since a purely secular philosophy can confuse one's understanding of reality and of life, a Christian philosophy becomes necessary in order to explicate, clarify, and communicate the essentials of a world-and-life view implicit in the Christian revelation.

3. One means for such clarification and communication has been the drawing of analogies to current concepts by an incisive adaptation of word meanings. This involves using the philosophical tools of a given culture. Whereas the rationalist and liberal traditions modified Christian concepts and adapted them to cultural uses, the Biblical writers modified cultural concepts and adapted them to Christian use.

Further Implications

COMMON GROUND

The use of current philosophical tools, whether for clarification or for communication, requires that we identify the common ground between believers and unbelievers which makes it possible. We suggest that such common ground is of two kinds: the generic, which is common to all men, and the cultural, which is common within a given culture. Generic likenesses have traditionally been rooted in the fact that all men are created in the image of God. In that all are rational creatures, they have in common an obligation to the basic laws of thought; no man can equivocate or contradict himself while thinking properly. In that all are moral creatures, they have in common an obligation to moral law. Whether or not they recognize the law of God, there persists some sense of "oughtness" related to basic areas of value which all men share—areas such as the family, property, physical well-being, etc.—in the context of which different cultures formulate their moral codes. In that all are similarly constituted psychologically, all men have in common certain basic needs, the satisfaction of which is one of life's greatest demands. Undoubtedly the rational, moral, and psychological are all closely interrelated, and further categories could probably be added, but the generic similarities found in such traits as these provide a common basis that facilitates the Christian use of the philosophical stock in trade of the non-Christian world. They provide a partial basis for mutual understanding and communication.

We say "partial" advisedly. Christian theology asserts that the image of God in man is distorted by sin. In so far as this affects non-Christian rationality, moral sensitivity, and psychological needs—to use the examples selected above—the common ground is disturbed. It should be noted, however, that while human depravity extends into all areas of the personality, it does not totally destroy normal human traits. Prior commitments, sinful attitudes, godless motivation indeed corrupt them. A man's reasoning processes will accordingly be distorted, and more so in closer proximity to the crucial issue of the knowledge of God in Christ. But he can never escape his obligation to the laws of thought; nonsense is still nonsense and error is still error. Moreover, his moral sensitivity may be dulled and his moral code distorted, but he remains a moral being with recognized obligations. He may repress his basic psychological needs or seek satisfaction for them in godless ways that build in him a grossly distorted personality, but the needs persistently exhibit themselves in life's frustrations, tensions, and psychoses. In other words, regardless of all the distortion of the image of God, a man remains a man. God does not allow His creation to be corrupted beyond measure. He preserves sufficient common ground to make possible both communication and understanding.

Cultural likenesses exist among members of the same culture. Western culture, in the Greco-Roman tradition as affected by the Hebrew-Christian religions, provides common ground for mutual understanding and communication. Oriental cultures provide the same. Within common cultures communication and understanding are easier than between different cultures. To the extent, then, that Christians are members of a given culture they are thereby enabled to use the tools of that culture in orienting Christianity to prevailing thought-patterns. Here is common ground.

There is a sense in which the Christian does not fit his culture. His ideas and values, being Biblically based, are often at variance with those of unredeemed men and an unredeemed culture. This, however, does not gainsay the obvious, that he is still compelled to make use of the tools of his culture in explicating and expressing his faith. After all, he has no tools other than these.

THE PRIMACY OF REVELATION

The apostolic use of current philosophical tools is to be distinguished from that of a Marcion or even a Justin Martyr. Whereas the latter tended to conform Christian ideas to the cultural, the apostles sought to adapt the cultural to the Christian. It is here that historic orthodoxy parts company with modern liberalism. The liberal was willing to dispense with Biblical concepts—whether of the trinity or of the atonement or of eschatology—in order to make his message acceptable in his culture. Even a Tillich and a Niebuhr radically alter the Biblical concepts of sin and grace in adapting to the existential mood. The conservative, on the other hand, insists with Augustine and the Reformers on the primacy of revelation; the Scriptures are his final and sufficient rule of both faith and practice. If current con-

cepts and moods differ from the Biblical, then they are
at fault and must be corrected. If they are analogous
to the Biblical, then they may be carefully employed
in the explication of Christian thought.

This may readily be illustrated. Take the Marxist
view of history. Its economic determinism claims that
all phases of human life are and always have been gov-
erned by the economic forces that produce class war-
fare. The Christian philosopher disagrees. While he
cannot deny that economic forces have played a significant part in history, and especially since the Industrial
Revolution, yet from an objective viewpoint he sees history as an extremely complex process. To single out
economic causes above all others is an oversimplifica-
tion; the "proof" offered by Marx and Lenin suffers from
incomplete induction and amounts to a hasty general-
ization. Our philosopher finds man's rational, moral, and
spiritual characteristics hard to account for within the
limits of a Marxist behaviorism. He finds in Christianity's doctrine of the image of God and its distortion by
sin a preferable perspective from which to understand
both the uniqueness of man and the regrettable class
struggle. As a Christian, moreover, he has come to regard the complexities of history as somehow reflecting
the providential activity of his God. From starting points
such as these he approaches the philosophy of history
with its concomitant problems in ethics and metaphysics.

But beyond a certain point his commitment to the
primacy of revelation does not as clearly lead him.
Christianity indeed claims to meet the basic needs of

men. But this does not mean that every intellectual perplexity is *ipso facto* dispelled. The precise philosophical expression of the nature of man, the relationship of mind to matter, the extent of environmental influence on human behavior, the degree of objectivity available in historical knowledge, the choice between divergent views of the a priori—in these and other questions the decision of the Christian philosopher becomes as much or even more a matter of philosophical preference as of religious commitment. He could hardly be a materialist, it is true, but he could conceivably be either an idealist or a dualist. He could hardly be a deist but might follow either Aquinas or Kant in the value ascribed to the theistic arguments. He may come to regard his particular view of historical knowledge or of the theistic arguments as more useful to the Christian apologist, or even as more consistent with his particular tradition within the Christian religion; but in these more debatable matters his commitment is made more on philosophic than on Biblical grounds. Christianity gives considerable direction and motivation to philosophy. But it is not a philosophy, nor does its revelation lead unequivocally to the sort of closed and dogmatic system which modern existentialism and analysis despise. One cannot infer from Christian premises conclusive answers to every philosophical problem. It is for this reason that even Christian philosophers differ. Their philosophies, like those of their non-Christian colleagues, reflect a variety of influences and viewpoints. They, too, are engaged in the quest for a degree of clarity and the kind of a system that may for the present remain elusive.

THE CHRISTIAN PHILOSOPHER

What, then, is the function of the Christian in philosophy? A threefold answer is possible. First, the Christian philosopher may serve theology. Sir William Hamilton once asserted that "no difficulty emerges in theology which has not previously emerged in philosophy." If this is so, the Christian philosopher will contribute to the discussion of theological problems old and new a penetrating insight, which will not only help him distinguish truth from error, but also enable him to understand the truth in terms that are meaningful to the contemporary mind. He will avoid the obscurity of hackneyed clichés and of terms now ambiguous or passé; and, as was done in historical discussions of the Trinity, the origin of the human soul, and so forth, he will bring to the work of systematization the tools of philosophy.

The Christian philosopher may also serve apologetics; in doing so he will speak, not to the church as he does in theology, but to the world. He will strive for a clarity of understanding, a consistency of argument, and a contemporaneity of expression which, by humble dependence on the illuminating power of the Holy Spirit, will commend the faith to the secular mind. He will seek to show that Christianity is intellectually respectable, that it is relevant, that it is defensible, that it is the most appealing of all the voices which clamor for the ears of contemporary man.

Finally, the Christian philosopher may serve his culture. Here he does what any philosopher does, but he does it as a Christian. The philosopher, we have observed, serves two functions: by his quest for clarity he serves as an intellectual conscience; by developing a coherent world view he serves as a cultural guide. The Christian philosopher, benefiting from the light of revelation and seeking clarity of understanding on the same philosophical problems as his non-Christian colleague, provides a Christian intellectual conscience for his age. He will, perhaps, be most concerned about confusions and inconsistencies in areas that bear directly on the faith: views of man and God, of truth, beauty, and goodness. But by his quest for clarity in all things he bears witness to the concern of the Christian faith and life for every perplexity of the human mind.

The Christian philosopher, moreover, will want to develop as far as he can a Christian world-and-life view—one which sees life steadily, as a whole, and from the perspective of Biblical revelation. His epistemology will take into account the place of faith and revelation; his metaphysics will be guided by his theism with its doctrine of creation; his ethics will embrace the law of God and Christ's redemption; his philosophy of history will see the world process as moving under the providence of the Judge of all men. But he will not confine himself to translating theology into philosophical language. Rather he will try to incorporate these Christian ideas and values that are also discussed in theology into the broader scope of a system that respects also materials and problems which are common to a given culture or to men generically. From this perspective he may speak to his day, seeking as do other philosophers to shed light on the varied problems and changing structures of human experience. He will stand a responsible member of society, sensitive in soul and alert to the bewildering conflicts of an onrushing history. He will come, not to be ministered unto, but to minister.

J. V. L. Casserley expresses it succinctly in his work *The Christian in Philosophy:*

> ... this is the high prophetic office of a Christian philosopher, but it is one that can only be fulfilled by a Christian philosophy so rigorously philosophical that the most obstinately "pure" philosopher will admit it to his discussions, and at the same time so manifestly a way of grace that the simplest and most unphilosophical Christian will remember it in his prayers.[1]

[1] Published by Charles Scribner's Sons, New York, 1951, page 262. Quoted by permission.

SUGGESTED FURTHER READINGS

The following list, though somewhat arbitrary, is intended to represent significant contributions to an understanding of the problem as a whole. The most significant omissions are the writings of recent individual proponents such as Van Til and Dooyeweerd, or Brunner and Ferré.

AUGUSTINE. "Of True Religion" and "The Usefulness of Belief." These are his two essays dealing most explicitly with the issue raised by the rationalism of the Manicheans. Both are available in the volume, *Augustine: Earlier Writings*, ed. J. H. S. Burleigh. Philadelphia: Westminster Press, 1953.

AQUINAS, THOMAS. *Summa Contra Gentiles*, Vol. I, sections 1-8. The classical statement of the Thomistic synthesis of faith and reason. Augustine and Aquinas stand as landmarks in the history of Christian thought.

CASSERLEY, J. V. L. *The Christian in Philosophy*. New York: Charles Scribner's Sons, 1951. A historical approach to the contemporary problem. A most helpful study by an Anglican scholar, somewhat technical, very up-to-date, focusing on the function of Christian philosophers.

The Christian Scholar, XXXIX (March, 1956), 87-163. A series of helpful articles discussing explicitly the relationship of Christianity and philosophy.

CLARK, GORDON H. *A Christian View of Men and Things.* Grand Rapids: Wm. B. Eerdmans Publishing Company, 1952. One of America's leading evangelical philosophers argues the superiority of a Christian world view over its contemporary rivals. This is the Christian at work in philosophy for apologetic purposes.

GILSON, ETIENNE. *Reason and Revelation in the Middle Ages.* New York: Charles Scribner's Sons, 1938. A contemporary Thomistic scholar lucidly traces the problem from its inception in patristic times. An introductory treatment which brings the medieval positions into focus.

NIEBUHR, RICHARD. *Christ and Culture.* New York: Harper & Brothers, 1951. A brilliant discussion of a broader issue, focusing on five viewpoints: radical, accommodationist, synthesist, dualist, and conversionist.

RAMM, BERNARD. *Types of Apologetic Systems.* Grand Rapids: Baker Book House, 1953. A useful survey of three types of approach to a more limited question: apologetic positions stressing subjective immediacy, natural theology, and revelation.

WILD, JOHN. *Human Freedom and Social Order.* Durham, N. C.: Duke University Press, 1959. A distinguished American philosopher discusses in existentialist terms the role of a Christian orientation in philosophy, providing a "guiding image" for intellectual inquiry.

YOUNG, WARREN C. *A Christian Approach to Philosophy.* Grand Rapids: Baker Book House, 1954. An evangelical introduction to various philosophical problems and positions. Written as a textbook, it surveys issues and suggests Christian perspectives.